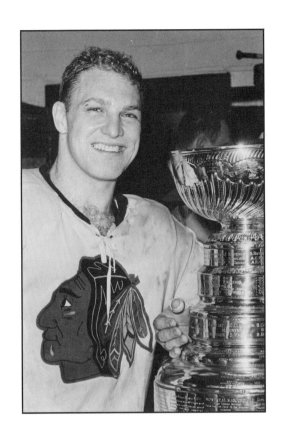

Center Troy Murray, one of the talented young stars on today's Chicago Blackhawks.

BLACKHAWKS
CHICAGO

BY ROSS RENNIE

CREATIVE EDUCATION INC.

Published by Creative Education, Inc.
123 S. Broad Street, Mankato, Minnesota 56001

Designed by Rita Marshall
Photos by Bruce Bennett Studios,
Frank Howard/Protography and Wide World Photos

Library of Congress Cataloging-in-Publication Data

Rennie, Ross.
  The Chicago Blackhawks/by Ross Rennie.
    p.   cm.
    Summary: Presents, in text and illustrations, the history of
the Chicago Blackhawks hockey team.
    ISBN 0-88682-276-9
    1. Chicago Blackhawks (Hockey team)—History—Juvenile literature.
[1. Chicago Blackhawks (Hockey team)—History.   2. Hockey—History.]
I. Title.
GV848.C48R45   1989
796.96′264′0977311—dc20

                                                        89-37731
                                                              CIP
                                                               AC

THE BEGINNINGS: 1926–1956

Founded less than 200 years ago, the city of Chicago has had a short but colorful history. The "Great Chicago Fire of 1871," which started, according to legend, when a cow owned by Mrs. Patrick O'Leary kicked over a lighted lantern, devastated Chicago's central business district. The flames killed at least 300 people and destroyed $200 million worth of property. In the 1920s and early 1930s gangsters such as Al Capone and other underworld figures gave Chicago a reputation for crime and violence in numerous battles over the United States' prohibition laws.

Dick Irvin was named the Blackhawks' first captain in 1926.

The Blackhawks defeated the Detroit Red Wings for their first Stanley Cup championship.

Since then, Chicago has grown up into one of the world's greatest cities. Urban renewal projects and commitments to industry have made Chicago the business and transportation capital of the midwestern United States. Chicago also has become a cultural center with many museums, parks and sporting events to entertain its more than 7 million citizens. During the cold winter months, these activities are highlighted by the fast-paced action held in Chicago Stadium, the home of the National Hockey League's (NHL) Chicago Blackhawks.

Like Chicago itself, the Blackhawks have had a colorful history. The "Curse of Muldoon," a hex which was placed on the team in 1927 by former coach Pete Muldoon to prevent them from ever finishing in first place, held true until 1967, an amazing forty years later. In 1957 Hawk star Bill Mosienko led a group nicknamed the "Pony Line." They established a league record that still stands today, by scoring three goals in 21 seconds.

This colorful and exciting team began play in the NHL in 1926. The early years of the team were marked by poor records and dismal performances. But by the 1933–34 season the Blackhawks had improved enough to capture their first league championship with a victory over a strong Detroit Red Wing club. This victory, which earned them the Stanley Cup trophy, was due in large part to the great goaltending of Charlie Gardiner.

Gardiner was the captain of the Blackhawk team and was the league's premier goaltender through the early 1930s. In 1934, when the league was committed to a 48 game schedule, Gardiner established an NHL single season mark of 10 shutouts. Gardiner was a dedicated hockey

During the 1980's Doug Wilson and the Blackhawks struggled to relive the championship days of 1934.

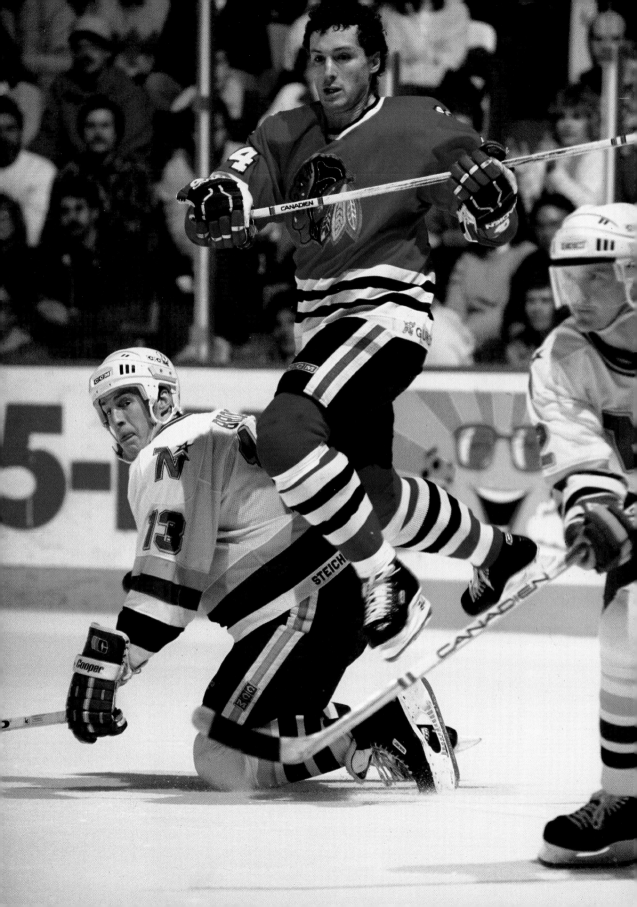

Sam Lo Presti took over the job as the Blackhawks number one goaltender.

professional. Coach Bill Tobin, who directed Chicago for 30 years, commented that, "Hockey was Gardiner's life."

Unfortunately, shortly after the Hawks had won their first Stanley Cup, Gardiner's life came to a tragic end when he suffered a fatal brain hemorrhage.

Replacing Gardiner in the nets was difficult. For the next three years the Blackhawks struggled. By 1938, however, they had regained their championship form and brought to Chicago their second Stanley Cup trophy in four years.

The next fifteen years brought troubled times to the world. A time when the emphasis on sports and entertainment took a backseat to global conflicts and regional confrontations. Through it all, the NHL and the Blackhawks continued, but their outcomes seemed to take on less importance.

As a hockey club these were troublesome years for the Blackhawks as well. Poor records and low attendance contributed to Chicago's woes. There were, however, several highlights during this period that helped sustain the team.

A year after the Blackhawks had won their second Stanley Cup, team owner Major McLaughlin introduced a unique idea to his club. McLaughlin gave the order to have his entire team made up of American players. After implementing this concept the Blackhawks, only a year after being the best team in hockey, won just one of their first six games and finished in last place in the league. McLaughlin's idea was quickly abandoned and has never again been tried in the NHL.

The Blackhawks best season during the 1940s was 1943–44. That year the Hawks made it all the way to the Stanley Cup finals before losing to the Montreal Canadiens in four straight games. The team was led by the Bentley brothers, Max and Doug. Although both were small and lightweight their speed and quickness enabled them to make a tremendous impact on Chicago and the NHL.

Each player, at one point in his career, led the National Hockey League in scoring. They are the only pair of brothers to have accomplished this feat in the history of the NHL. During one stretch another brother, Reg, joined Doug and Max in Chicago where all three played on the same line, another NHL first.

But even the talented Bentleys could not lift the Blackhawks for long. Soon the team was again struggling to make it out of last place in the standings.

1 9 4 3

Max Bentley won the Lady Byng Award for the NHL's Most Gentlemanly Player.

THE EXPANSION YEARS: 1957–1969

In 1957, however, the fortunes of the Blackhawk franchise would begin to change. The man responsible for the turnaround was Robert Martin Hull. Bobby Hull, or the "Golden Jet" as he became known to his fans, was born January 3, 1939 in Pointe Anne, Ontario, Canada. From the early age of ten when he played his first Bantam game; to the age of 18 when Hull played his first professional game as a Blackhawk, most people knew he was a special hockey player. Bob Wilson, who was the chief scout for the Blackhawks, first saw Hull play when he was just in his teens. "He (Hull) had the skills of an experienced pro at the age of 14," Wilson commented, we could have used him then . . ."

Indeed, the Hawks needed Hull. In the past four years they had come in last place in the NHL. They had not won the Stanley Cup since 1938. The stands in Chicago Stadium were seldom filled.

"The Golden Jet," Bobby Hull, led the Blackhawks into the 1960s.
(pages 10–11)

9

A toothless Bobby Hull celebrated a Chicago victory.

In Hull's first three seasons with the Hawks the team improved to gain two third place finishes. But by Hull's fourth year as a pro, the team was ready to mature. Bobby by this time had physically developed into the league's most dominant player.

At 5' 10" and 195 pounds, he was one of the strongest players in hockey. With his tremendous strength Hull made popular the slap shot. Winding the stick high above his head, he would swing it down in an instant, shooting the puck up to 118 miles per hour. Using his strong legs Hull was also the fastest player in the game, often traveling down the ice at 44 feet per second.

Hull's speed and power proved to be a lethal combination for his opponents. People who tried to defense him, if they could catch him, would often just bounce off Hull. A player from another team commented, "checking Hull is like crashing into cement." In an attempt to slow down the "Golden Jet" opponents began to trip him and hold onto his arms. He was the most feared offensive player in hockey.

All the attention on the ice tired Hull. "You turn away from one man and there's another on you," he said, "but I'm up to the challenge." And Hull proved it, even when injured the Hawks could count on Bobby Hull. "As long as Bobby can stand up," remarked Chicago coach Billy Reay, "he wants to be out there on the ice."

This attitude was the hallmark of Bobby's career in Chicago. Not only would it help him set numerous individual records, including becoming the first player to score more than 50 goals in a season, 1965–66. It helped him make the Blackhawks a legitimate Stanley Cup contender.

So as Hull developed, so too did the Blackhawks. By the 1960–61 season they had become the elite team of the NHL. That season saw the Stanley Cup return to Chicago for the first time in 23 years. After defeating the Montreal Canadiens in the semifinal round of the playoffs, the Hawks advanced to the finals against the powerful Detroit Red Wings.

The series also matched two of the greatest hockey players of all-time against one another, Bobby Hull of Chicago versus Gordie Howe of the Red Wings. But it was the strength of Hull's supporting cast that brought the Cup back to Chicago. Players such as Stan Mikita, Glenn Hall and Pierre Pilote made major contributions. In critical game 5 of the series Chicago center Stan Mikita scored two goals to lift Chicago to a 6–3 victory and give the Blackhawks an unsurmountable advantage in the series.

Mikita, who by many was considered the best center in

1 9 6 0

Bobby Hull led the Blackhawks in scoring with eighty-one points.

13

Goalie Glenn Hall rejoiced as Chicago won their first Stanley Cup title in twenty-three years.

hockey during the 1960s, was born Stanislas Gvoth. Following the communist takeover of their country in 1948, his parents decided their son would be better off outside of the country. As a result Stan, as he would later be known, was adopted by his aunt and uncle, Joe and Anna Mikita, and moved to St. Catharines, Ontario.

Considering the public recognition given to Hull during Mikita's NHL career, it is easy to overlook his contributions to the team. But when looking back at his record one can not underestimate his value. Coach Billy Reay made this assessment of Mikita, "he has Rocket Richard's accuracy as a shooter, Gordie Howe's defensive mastery, Bobby Hull's speed and shot, and Jean Bealiveau's stick-handling ability. Mikita does more with everything he's got than any other player I've seen."

As a testament to his ability, Mikita to this day still holds Blackhawk records for most seasons played, 21; most games played, 1394; most career assists, 926; and most career points, 1467. In addition to his team records he is the only NHL player to ever win the Hart Trophy (Most Valuable Player), the Lady Byng Trophy (Best Sportsmanship), and the Art Ross Trophy (Leading Point Scorer) in one year. And Stan accomplished the feat two consecutive years.

With Mikita and Hull leading the way, and the addition of talented newcomers such as Phil Esposito, Chico Maki and Bobby Hull's younger brother Dennis, the Blackhawks were one of the dominant teams in the NHL through the early and middle 1960s. Besides winning the Stanley Cup in 1961, they reached the Stanley Cup finals in 1962–63 facing the Toronto Maple Leafs. During the 1966–67 season Chicago compiled the best record in their

Although sometimes overshadowed by Bobby Hull, Stan Mikita was one of hockey's greatest stars.

history. But beginning with a disappointing opening round loss to the Toronto Maple Leafs in the 1967 playoffs, the fortunes of the Blackhawks began to stumble.

The next misfortune occurred when Chicago management traded the young Phil Esposito. In a deal that sent Esposito, Ken Hodge and Fred Stanfield to the Boston Bruins for Gilles Marotte, Pit Martin and Jack Norris, the Blackhawks, in effect, sacrificed their future. A Toronto Star sports editor described it as the worst trade in the history of hockey from Chicago's standpoint. Team captain Bobby Hull remarked that Esposito had been one of the reasons for his success, "he was my right arm," Bobby said.

Together Bobby Hull (above) and Stan Mikita (right) formed a dangerous tandem in the 1960s and 70s.

Phil Esposito's younger brother Tony joined the Blackhawks as a goaltender in 1969. (pages 18–19)

One constant during the 1970s was the outstanding play of Tony Esposito.

MORE CHANGES: THE DECADE OF THE SEVENTIES

The decade of the seventies was a period of change in the National Hockey League. Expansion pushed the number of teams competing for the Stanley Cup from six to twenty. A rival professional league, the World Hockey Association, was formed in 1972. The changes affected every team in the NHL, but none more so than the Chicago Blackhawks.

Having traded the majority of their young talent away in the 1967 deal with Boston, the Blackhawks counted heavily upon the veteran leadership of Bobby Hull and Stan Mikita. Consequently, the events of the summer of 1972 shook the foundation of the Chicago franchise.

That was the year the WHA was formed. The league began with teams in Chicago, Boston, Ottawa, Winnipeg and several other locations. Initially, the league had difficulties, as the lack of star players hurt attendance. They needed a proven player to join their league with the hope that others would follow. To solve the problem, each team in the new league put money into a "star fund." The sum totaled $1,000,000. The star they offered this money to was Chicago's Bobby Hull.

Hull, who was having contract problems with Blackhawk owner Bill Wirtz, jumped at the offer. In addition to the upfront money, Hull also received a guaranteed $1.7 million contract to play for the Winnipeg Jets.

1 9 7 3

Keith Magnuson's competitive spirit helped the Blackhawks reach the Stanley Cup finals.

The loss of Hull was devastating to Chicago. Although they were able to reach the Stanley Cup finals in 1973 behind the strong play of Stan Mikita, this would be the end of Chicago's days as a NHL power.

Chicago's roster was growing old. Only four players that started the decade of the seventies on the Blackhawk's roster remained at the end of the 1979 season. This high turnover contributed to the team's poor play. Although they did manage to win the West division in 1979, this was the lone highlight of an up and down decade for the Chicago Blackhawks.

One constant, however, was the superb play of their goalie Tony Esposito. Known to his fans as "Tony O," Esposito was the younger brother of former Blackhawk Phil Esposito. His route to Chicago, unlike his brother's, was long and adventurous.

After graduating from Michigan Tech in 1967, where he had led his college hockey team to an NCAA championship as a sophomore and had been selected as an All-American for three consecutive years, Tony was drafted by the Montreal Canadiens. After three years of hard luck and travel-

Like Esposito, Denis Savard became a Chicago Blackhawk superstar.

ing between the Canadiens and their minor league team, Esposito's fortunes changed.

In 1969 Tony was selected by the Blackhawks in the annual NHL minor league draft. The Hawks, having recently lost their star goalie Glenn Hall, were in need of help and Esposito was the solution.

In his rookie season the awkward goaltender from Sault Sainte Marie, Ontario, became an instant superstar. During the course of the year Esposito recorded 15 shutouts, a new NHL record; won the Vezina trophy, an award given to the goaltender, or team of goalies, who have the lowest goals against average for the year; and was also named the NHL Rookie of the Year.

Tony Esposito won his third Vezina Trophy, the award given to the NHL's outstanding goalie.

His critics, who only a year earlier were saying his sprawling style would never make it in the NHL, were silenced. His exceptionally quick reflexes and ability to cover the angles had made him one of the NHL's elite goalies in just his first complete season as a professional. Now any references to his style were quickly quieted by Tony O with his casual response, "I thought the object was to stop the puck, not look beautiful doing it."

Over the next decade Tony Esposito continued his excellence for the Blackhawks and earned him the reputation of being one of the best goaltenders in the history of hockey. Despite having only average talent around him, Esposito singlehandedly kept his team in playoff contention throughout the 1970s and early 1980s.

(clockwise): Denis Savard, Doug Wilson, Al Secord, Darryl Sutter.

TODAY'S CHICAGO BLACKHAWKS:
THE 1980S AND BEYOND

Similar to the 1960s, when Chicago faced the difficult task of rebuilding their hockey club, the 1980s brought a time of upheaval to the Blackhawks. Both eras were preceded by relatively unsuccessful years. The changes of the 1960s brought Bobby Hull and a Stanley Cup championship to Chicago. The changes of the 1980s, however, were not nearly as successful.

The individual responsible for rebuilding the Blackhawks of the 1980s was general manager and coach Bob Pulford. As a player, Pulford was recognized throughout the NHL as a defensive-style forward for the Toronto Maple Leafs. As a coach and general manager, his teams took on a much different look.

Beginning with the 1980 NHL entry draft, Pulford set out to transform the Blackhawks into an aggressive offensive unit. Acquiring Denis Savard, Steve Ludzik, Steve Larmer and Troy Murray in the annual selection process went a long way to accomplishing this goal.

Of these four players, Savard and Murray best exemplified the Blackhawks changing image. Denis Savard, nicknamed "Saavy," was a quick, exciting player from Pointe Gatineau, Quebec. As the Hawks number one pick in the 1980 draft, much was expected of him. His performance did nothing to disappoint his teammates or his fans. With the ability to execute all his moves at top speed and his unmatched acceleration, Savard would remind many of the great Bobby Hull. During his career he would go on to break several of Hull's records including most points as a rookie, and most points in a season.

1 9 8 0

Steve Ludzik was Chicago's second round pick, twenty-eighth overall, in the amateur draft.

Darryl Sutter served as the Blackhawk captain from 1982–1987.
(pages 26–27)

1 9 8 3

*Orvel Tessier was
named the NHL's
Coach of the Year.*

Overshadowed by the flashy style of Savard was Troy Murray. Troy was the 51st player taken in the 1980 entry draft. After leading the University of North Dakota hockey team to the NCAA championship in 1982, Murray joined the Blackhawks.

"When I first saw him as a teenager, I had absolutely no indication he would become this type of player, said assistant general manager Jack Davison. "But after watching Troy in the NCAA tournament, we knew we had ourselves a prize. Not only was he the best player on the ice, but he was also made the captain of the team, that tells you something."

With Savard and Murray as the nucleus of a powerful offensive attack the Blackhawks seemed poised for greatness. In addition, Chicago obtained Al Secord in a trade with the Boston Bruins giving them added muscle to their lineup.

Unfortunately, the increased offensive production led to a decline in their defensive play. In 1980–81, for the first time in their 50 year history, Chicago allowed over 300 goals in a season. Over the next nine years they would repeat this infamous feat six times.

The lack of defense, combined with frequent injuries, resulted in only three winning seasons during the 1980s. This decade was highlighted by the 1982–83 season, when Orvel Tessier led the Hawks to a 104 point season and was named the NHL's Coach of the Year.

Despite their poor records, Chicago still managed to qualify for the playoffs each year during the 1980s. In fact they managed to qualify for the semifinal round of the playoffs three times. Each fact being a direct benefit of

*Troy Murray has been a steady performer for the Blackhawks since he
joined the team in 1981.*

30   *The slick passing Steve Larmer holds the Chicago single season assist record.*

Mike Keenan, shown here addressing his players, was named the Blackhawks' head coach on June 9, 1988.

playing in the NHL's Norris division, the weakest in professional hockey.

By the end of the 1987–88 season, Pulford and Blackhawk management had become disgruntled with the team's lack of development. In an effort to improve the club, they hired Mike Keenan, a tough, defensive minded leader, as the 28th coach in the team's 63 year history. Keenan had previously coached the Philadelphia Flyers for four seasons.

As coach of the Blackhawks, his job was to restore the pride and the winning tradition of Chicago into the 1990s. Keenan was philosophical in his approach. "All you can do is keep educating and teaching the player," he said. "Hopefully they'll get the message. I see signs of improvement everyday," Keenan added, "they're just not coming fast enough."

With the help of players such as Denis Savard, Troy Murray, Keith Brown, Doug Wilson, Duane Sutter and Rick Vaive, coach Keenan has the talent to develop a winning hockey team. But it will take patience for the Blackhawks to become a legitimate contender for Lord Stanley's Cup. A prize that the Blackhawks have not won since 1961. But a prize that Blackhawk players, and fans alike, will cherish all the more.

1 9 8 8

After nine years with the Blackhawks Keith Brown recorded his 250th career point.